Not Afraid!

Not Afraid!

Thoughts on Fearless Living

Wilson O. Weldon

The Upper Room
Nashville, Tennessee

Not Afraid!

Cover design: Linda Bryant
Book design: Harriette Bateman
First printing: May, 1984 (5)
Library of Congress Catalog Card No: 83-51400
ISBN 0-8358-0482-8

To

Terry Sanford

*Courageous Governor of North Carolina,
Fearless President, Builder of a Greater Duke University,
Unashamedly Related to the Church*

Acknowledgments

"The Little man Who Wasn't There" by Hughes Mearns. Used by permission of Mrs. Petra Cabot.

"This, Too, Will Pass" from *Light of the Years* by Grace Noll Crowell. © 1936 by Harper & Row, Inc.. Renewed 1964 by Grace Noll Crowell. Reprinted by permission of Harper & Row Publishers.

Scripture quotations designated KJV are from the King James Version of the Bible.

Scripture quotations designated RSV are from the Revised Standard Version of the Bible, copyrighted 1946, 1952 and © 1971 by the Division of Christian Education, National Council of the Churches of Christ in the United States of America, and are used by permission.

Scripture quotations designated NEB are from *The New English Bible*, © The Delegates of the Oxford University Press and the Syndics of the Cambridge University Press 1961 and 1970, are reprinted by permission.

Scripture quotations designated TEV are from the *Good News Bible, The Bible in Today's English Version*, copyright by American Bible Society 1966, 1971, © 1976, and are used by permission.

For Some

Meaninglessness has a strong grip;
Nothing delights them very deeply;
Hopes and dreams do not
   reach beyond the next holiday;
Work is pointless and boring.

—W.O.W.

Others

Are held in the grip of everyday
   routines; afraid that life will end before
   they have discovered a
   meaning to their days.

—W.O.W.

The Unafraid

'Twas grace that taught my heart to fear,
And grace my fears relieved. . . .
. . . 'Tis grace hath brought me safe thus far,
And grace will lead me home.

—John Newton

Contents

Not Afraid!

Foreword

Courage is an essential ingredient if one is to live successfully. Courage is a virtue that all of us see exemplified in our classical past. It was one of the cardinal virtues of ancient Greek and Roman society. Likewise, it is a virtue in Christian society.

The difference is that courage when modified by Christianity is not animal daring or the foolhardiness of physical strength. Rather it is spiritual endurance, and it has a kinship to perseverance.

"Blessed are you," Jesus said, "when men shall revile you, and persecute you, and say all manner of evil against you falsely, for my sake. . . . be exceeding glad . . . for so persecuted they the prophets which were before you" (Matt. 5:11-12, KJV). John F. Kennedy, as a young senator, wrote his book, *Profiles in Courage*, which won the Pulitzer Prize. Wilson Weldon has written another book which might well be entitled, *Profiles in Christian Courage*. Unlike Kennedy, he does not deal in biographies. Rather he delineates his theme through topics. In this way, he deals with courage in the life of each of us. He makes us see ourselves when we lack it. He gives us strength to pray for it. And he enables us to exercise it by the power of divine grace.

Wilson Weldon is a master of illustration. Perhaps he learned this from his old mentor, Dr. G. Ray Jordan. He more than anyone else has succeeded Dr. Jordan as one of the masters of the contemporary pulpit. We have not had in the ministry of the southeastern jurisdiction of the United Methodist Church a more eloquent or more convincing preacher than Wilson Weldon.

Oftentimes, however, when one is able to preach from the pulpit, he is not able to express himself as vividly in type. This is not true of Wilson Weldon. Every chapter of this book rings as a sermon. It stirs the heart and quickens the mind. When one reads the pages, he can almost hear the words as if delivered from a pulpit.

Courage is not dealt with in terms of heroes. Rather courage is delineated in terms of the lives of ordinary, everyday people. The subtitle of the book is a description of its contents: "Thoughts on Fearless Living." Jesus tells us not to be anxious. But without him, every one of us is anxious most of the time. We can cope with today if we do not think about tomorrow. But when we begin to think what might occur tomorrow, anxieties rise like hideous giants to torment and frighten us. They can even destroy us, unless we acquire that courage which comes only through divine grace.

There is a progression of thought in this manuscript that is amazing to trace. It begins with the exclamation, "Not Afraid!" But then it tells us what we are to cope with in acquiring courage. We must not be afraid to be who we are, to believe what we must in order to love, to be an innovator, to speak out when danger strikes. But these things, wonderful as they are, are not enough. We must cope with loneliness, we must be able to handle whatever befalls us, we must face tomorrow as if we knew it in the complacency and serenity and competency of today. In the end this leads each of us to be a dreamer, and it brings us eventually to face the cross. Jesus, for the joy that was set before him, endured the cross for our sakes. And we must take our cross when it befalls us for the sake of others. This is the only way in which we can glorify God.

This is a beautiful and inspiring book. Every page has a message on it, and every sentence is a song.

I was impressed by the person to whom the book is dedicated, Terry Sanford. Mr. Sanford is not a preacher. He is a layman, a very accomplished and gifted layman, but one who has gone through ordinary experiences just like every one of us, and yet through it all has been a great governor of a great state and the leader and builder of a great Christian university.

I commend this book and give an unqualified recommendation.

BISHOP WILLIAM R. CANNON
Raleigh, North Carolina

1.

Not Afraid!

"Doctor, do you have any medicine for fear?" Seated in her doctor's office, a distraught, middle-aged widow listed one after another her many fears and anxieties. "Don't you have some medicine that will help me?"

If the average person is asked, "Have you ever been afraid?" surely the response would be yes. And certainly some fears are valid because part of our human nature is the instinctive emotion that warns us of physical danger. Often a life is rescued from death because of the normal, natural emotion of being afraid.

It is to the needless and foolish fears that we turn our thoughts, however. Too often phobias born of anxiety or depression weaken our whole being, stealing from us the chance to live happily and triumphantly. Being afraid without just reason is an illness, but it can be handled by those who bring it to God in faith, trusting that God will bring healing.

In the scriptures, fear is frequently mentioned. Over and over, Old Testament characters bring comfort and counsel under a banner of two words, *"Fear Not!"*

We should not confuse this affirmation with the frequent injunction in the Old Testament to "fear the Lord." "The fear of the Lord is the beginning of wisdom" (Psalm 111:10, KJV). "The fear of the Lord is clean, enduring forever" (Psalm 19:9, KJV). "The fear of the Lord is the fountain of life" (Prov. 14:27, NEB). This use of the word *fear* has a clear connotation of reverence for God, of a deep awe and admiration of God. To have such a genuine appreciation of God's majesty, power, and wisdom is to be wise. It does not negate the injunction to "fear not."

In the New Testament, Jesus as well as the early Christian leaders were face to face with danger and opposition so frequently that they might have surrendered. But New Testament scholars have often concluded that they constantly evidenced a convincing lack of fear—fear of poverty, of opposition, and even of death. Surely, an appropriate banner for the New Testament would be, "*Not Afraid!*"

So it is in this world of stress and strain that we need to pause and ponder the wisdom of developing a faith that can control the tendency to be afraid unnecessarily. Many persons can look back across their years and join in saying, "If I had my life to live over, I would not worry. Those fears and worries really never did me any good. I was foolish." Indeed, the tyrants which have ruled us so frequently have been *hurry* and *worry.* These give birth to foolish fears.

Wisdom belongs to the one who learns to distinguish between two kinds of fear: One that comes from reverence, and the other that springs from cowardice. The malady in most of us is that we have too little of the first, too much of the second. We falter, not when we are afraid, but when we are fearful of the wrong things. We do not fear God, but we are afraid of people. Instead of fearing sin, we are afraid of being found out.

Uncontrolled fear becomes the arch enemy of our finding a full and genuine personality. From such fear we learn worry, pessimism, greed, terror, and inferiority complexes. We lie awake at night dreading possible but unlikely calamities. We do and say cowardly things. We become selfish in dealing with others. Fear can even make us unwilling to stand up for what we believe.

What, then, is the medicine for this harmful and unnecessary disease?

One helpful way to handle our fears is to *face them pointedly and squarely.* Look at the facts, not the imaginations. Is there real truth in our fears, or are they lodged in untruth?

Once I was preparing to take my driver's license renewal test. I read the handbook and memorized the turns and highway signs. Soon I found myself thinking, *What if I don't pass? I will be humiliated. My wife will have to drive me everywhere I want to go.* Then, I backed myself into a corner and said, *If you fail, you can take it over. You have never failed the test before. Why should you flunk this time?* I overcame that imagined difficulty by looking at it squarely in the face.

We can learn to face difficulties and fears by carrying on in worthy pursuits, in doing what we can do wherever we are in whatever situation we may be. Sir Walter Scott was an example of this philosophy and strategy. In the midst of his writing successes, he was faced by financial losses and physical illness. He said of himself, "too exhausted to move, too giddy to read, too dizzy to listen, too confused to think." But he kept on. While writing the life of Napoleon, Scott commented, "My head aches, my eyes ache, my back aches—so does my breast—and I am sure my heart aches."[1] Yet, he was not afraid to continue writing.

At one time or another hard jobs confront us, bringing doubts about our ability. But we dare not sit down and whine. In lieu of fooling away precious moments in idleness, we can learn that inactivity breeds inability. The dark clouds of an unknown future tend to frighten us (we may lose our job; we may not be able to support the family). Then, as an act of our faith we need to bring a fresh and renewed commitment to doing what we can do now— remembering the truth in these two four-line stanzas:

> As I was going up the stair
> I met a man who wasn't there;
> He wasn't there again today!
> I wish, I *wish* he'd stay away.[2]
> —Hughes Mearns

and

> Some of your hurts you have cured,
> And the sharpest you still have survived,
> But what torments of grief you endured
> From evils that never arrived![3]
> —Ralph Waldo Emerson

Another helpful way to handle our fears is to remember that *most situations (not all) which appear to be frightening are shortlived.* If we think of what the worst result could be, and then couple it with what the best would be, we will soon have it all in a clearer perspective.

Someone has reported that during the First World War, when the airplane was still in its infancy stage, many fears loomed before the army fliers. Soon there developed a common saying among the fliers that went like this: When you are in the air, you will be either flying straight or turning over. If you are flying straight, there is no cause for worry. If you are turning over, one of two things is true: you will either right the plane or fall. If you right the plane, there is no cause for worry. If you fall, one of two things is certain: you will be either injured slightly or injured seriously. If you are injured slightly, there is no cause for worry. If you are injured seriously, one of two things will happen: you will either die or recover. If you recover, there is no cause for worry. And if you die, you can't worry anyway. How curiously true that is!

In my early years, my widowed mother, when facing a problem, often said, "This, too, will pass away." That statement made an impact upon me as a boy, and it has often strengthened me in later years. No matter how frightening a time may be, "it, too, will pass away."

> This, too, will pass. Oh, heart, say it over and over
> Out of your deepest sorrow, out of your grief,

No hurt can last forever, perhaps tomorrow
Will bring relief.

This, too, will pass. It will spend itself, its fury
Will die as the wind dies down at the set of sun;
Assuaged and calm you may rest at last, forgetting
A thing that is done.

Repeat it again and again, Oh, heart, for your comfort:
This, too, will pass, as surely as passed before
The old forgotten pain and the other sorrows
That once you bore.

As certain as stars at night or dawn after darkness,
Inherent as the lift of the blowing grass,
Whatever your despair or your frustration—
This, too, will pass.[4]

—Grace Noll Crowell

A third strategy in dealing with fears accents the assurance which every believer in Jesus Christ can and should have: *We are never alone.* Through the Holy Spirit, the Christ is here to hold us up and to embolden us, saying, "I am with you." "I will not leave you comfortless" (John 14:18, KJV). "My grace is sufficient for you" (2 Cor. 12:9, RSV). "I am with you alway, even unto the end of the world" (Matt. 28:20, KJV).

In opening prayers at church services, boards, and committees, many people have phrased this petition: "God, come into our midst," or "God, please be with us." That kind of prayer has disturbed me because I believe it portrays an unreality, a falsity. God is *already* with us in any time or place. How much more we need to pray, "God, make us *aware* of your presence! Enable us to respond to your vital relationships, and make them more meaningful to us."

What if you were in charge of a jail, and an earthquake opened the doors so that the prisoners could escape? Such an event is described beginning in Acts 16:25 when Paul and Silas were in prison. The fearful jailer was about to take his life when he cried, "What must I do to be saved?" Paul and Silas told him to believe in Jesus Christ. He did and he was restored. Such a simple thing to do, but how far-reaching! Belief in Jesus calls for faith that commits the whole self. One becomes like a passenger crossing the gangplank to board an ocean liner. Setting foot timidly on the deck, he or she soon feels the safety of the great ship. Faith in Jesus Christ does that exactly. We are carried by him who is able to take our life given by God to God.

That is a healing medicine for our fearful spirits! To know that when life forces us upon a stormy sea, when we must walk into a dark tunnel, or when we walk on a dark and unmarked road fearing all kinds of perils ahead—we are never alone!

2.

To Be Who I Am

In a conversation with a student on what we believe, especially in reference to William James' essay, "The Will to Believe," suddenly I was impressed by his comment, "If I only knew what makes me the way I am." That is a worthy thought because it centers on the question, "Who am I?"

A quick answer to this question can come from sociology with its emphasis on our many relationships, our environment, and our traditions. How our neighbors live, what our peers do and say—all of these help to make any of us the way we are.

Another valid answer comes from biology with its emphasis upon heredity and genetics. The genes given to us by our father and mother help to explain our body features and dispositions.

It is temptingly easy to stop and go no further. It is easy to get hung up on arguing which of these two is the strongest. John Gunther in *The Lost City* had a man to comment, when Hitler and the Nazis were rising in power, "It's the old question—what influences a person most, stomach or head?" A secularist or even an atheist can give these answers.

For a Christian believer there is much more. First, there must be a daring faith *to accept the fact that ours is a dual nature,* with an urge toward the good and a pull toward the bad. When Paul affirmed, "By the grace of God I am what I am" (1 Cor. 15:10, KJV), he pinpointed the ultimate power in the Christian's response to life. This gift of grace, of God's love, was not a unique gift to him

alone; it was a wonderful gift bestowed upon all who would receive
it.

In Romans 7:19 Paul admitted the fact of another side of his
makeup. Fearlessly he confessed, "The good that I would I do not:
but the evil which I would not, that I do" (KJV). What an insight, so
openly and bluntly described! "Who am I?" was answered by
describing that inner struggle, a civil war on the inside. God's grace
enabled Paul to overcome the pull of evil. And sooner or later every
Christian will face this dual pull. The incisive British chaplain
G. A. Studdert-Kennedy said it was this way:

> Our Padré says I'm a sinner,
>   And John Bull says I'm a saint,
> And they're both of 'em bound to be liars,
>   for I'm neither of them, I ain't.
> I'm a man, and a man's a mixture,
>   Right down from 'is very birth,
> For part ov 'im comes from 'eaven,
> And part of 'im comes from earth.[1]

Those who insist on "inevitable progress," as phrased by Her-
bert Spencer, or on the innate goodness of humankind without
facing the other nature do not fully understand the biblical picture.
It is a frightening sight—nuclear bombs and other technology have
exceeded our capacity to control them. Our basic goodness as
human beings is often thwarted by the demonic within us—the
greed, lust, and deceit which would undercut our ethical courage.
To keep our eyes open to this dangerous struggle is essential. It is a
long, daily struggle for individuals, and likewise for collective
society. It involves a continuing battle to overcome the corruption
of the human spirit and, by the grace of God, to change persons into
unselfish human beings dedicated to peace and unity among all
people.

Another understanding of who we are arises from the *direction
of our daily experiences*. No one can control totally what happens,

but the grace of the eternal God, when received, can enable us to control our responses to any happening. Whether or not our responses are to be self-centered, focusing upon ourselves only, will be a partial indicator of who is in control of our daily living. "In this world, and in this day, good moments go a long way for us, and the marvelous moment last Sunday when 1982's New York City Marathon winner Alberto Salazar, of Eugene, Oregon, before reaching for his warmup jacket, turned to the man just four seconds behind him, second-place finisher Rodolfo Gomez, of Delicias, Chihuahua, Mexico, and gave him a sustained hug has gone a much longer way for us than the Marathon's twenty-six-mile-three-hundred-and-eighty-five-yard course, and will last much longer than the two hours nine minutes and twenty-nine seconds it took for Salazar to reach the finish line."[2]

Only a hug, but how far it reached! Only a few moments, but there was the pointed direction of one's outreach, thoughtfulness, and compassion. Am I that kind of person very often in my daily runs? Who am I? What is the direction of my deeds?

Am I afraid to claim the power that comes directly from God into our being, enabling us to win over temptation to be less than our best selves:

—*When*, like the captive Jews in ancient Babylon we cry out, "How shall we sing the Lord's song in a strange land?" (Psalm 137:4, KJV).

—*When* in times of prosperity and success, arrogance and pride reach out to tempt us.

—*When* in days of adversity and privation we are besieged by despair and despondency.

—*When* in good moments of rightful joy we forget the old Jewish saying, "Each will have to give account of every good thing which he has refused to enjoy when he might have done so."

The kind of person I really want to be is directly related to how willing I am to accept God's power for my life. This is what Matthew Arnold called "the power not ourselves which makes for righteousness." When we are truly governed by God's grace is not when we say, "What a good boy am I." Instead, we know "not I, but the grace of God working with me." When my conscience is deeply troubled because of something I have done or failed to do, it is then I am aware not of my own goodness but of that power working within me.

A university student speaking at his graduation told about his father saying to him in his early years, "Son, courage is more than not being afraid. Real courage is when you face up to your failures, when you are willing to say, 'I didn't measure up.'" How frequently youth are urged toward success without the challenge to look for help in confronting their weaknesses and limitations.

The wise person admits that he or she is imperfect. If we take a straight, honest, and searching look at our real selves, we can discover not fear but power. A tragedy I have seen many times in counseling with men is a strong, almost resentful opposition to telling "the whole truth" about one's self. Until the *whole self* is confronted, there is small hope for finding the needed strength to win the battle with loss and defeat. An incident in the life of Jan Christiaan Smuts, the strong statesman in the early days of the Republic of South Africa, brings this point home. Smuts was nearing retirement when one day a French journalist approached him about writing the story of his life. Smuts agreed. At the interview Smuts stood up, looked at the lady, and said, "Here is my library, the files, records, diary. It is all for you to examine." Startled, the writer spoke, "But, sir, you did not really mean that I could go through *all* of your records. Surely you do have some secrets." "No," General Smuts replied, "there are no secrets."

That's the truth about everyone. In the final analysis, there are no secrets! We live, however, in a day when the role of *appearance* is accented. Things are made to look like something else—plastic to look like cloth, cloth to look like tile, tile to look like metal, metal to look like wood, and wood to look like plastic. That kind of subterfuge and pretense has no place in moral, Christian living.

Certainly it has no place in being unafraid to see who we really are!
I want to discover who I am. I want the strength to face that
reality. It will certainly lead me to an awareness that I am "of the
earth"—that I have sinned. I will confess my sin to God, believing
that God will hear and forgive me. Then, there can follow the
discovery that God does not want me to stay in the grip of my
weaknesses, but instead, to get on my feet, morally speaking, and
move forward with vigor and joy. Most of us are probably better
persons than we think we are—and the Creator wants us to find—
and enjoy—that better self.

In our days we are bombarded day and night with stories of
depravity, violence, and hatred. What a challenge it is to celebrate
the goodness and beauty we see in others. When we are shattered by
our own failures as well as by those we hear about, it is a grand,
ennobling thought to remember that there is another, even better
self wanting to be born.

There is a powerful scene in the life of Joan of Arc, as portrayed
in Lillian Hellman's drama, *The Lark*:

Joan:	I say that true miracles are not tricks performed by gypsies in a village square. True miracles are created by men when they use the courage and intelligence that God gave them.
Cauchon:	You are saying to us . . . that the real miracle of God on this earth is man. Man, who is naught but sin and error, impotent against his own wickedness—
Joan:	And man is also strength and courage and splendor in his most desperate minutes. I know man because I have seen him. He is a miracle.[3]

It all comes back to what Paul said: "By the grace of God I am
what I am." We can fearlessly face who we are if we will consciously live so that God's grace is the controlling power in our
lives.

3.

To Believe

One day a man who had suffered from ulcers for thirty years told his doctor that the only thing he asked of life was to be healed. "Suppose tomorrow you woke up cured—what would you do?" asked the forthright physician. "Why," the patient floundered, "I'd enjoy it, the way other people do." He was embarrassed because he was unable to be more specific.

Perhaps the real trouble with this man went deeper than his ulcers. He had no driving, compelling desire to get well in order to accomplish something which was most important to him!

What is our reason for living? This question brings another: What do I really, deep-down, believe?

Jesus called his followers by two names, "disciples" and "witnesses." In the Book of Acts the early Christians called themselves by another name, "believers." Acts 5:14 reads, "Numbers of men and women were added to their ranks as believers in the Lord" (NEB).

Our word *belief* or *believer,* as used in this text and in numerous other places in the New Testament, carries the idea of accepting statements, receiving certain propositions, holding specific convictions. This connotation may refer, for instance, to such an idea as the existence of God. Outright atheism was never a problem in the Old Testament. The Hebrews proudly accepted the idea that God existed, and so did the early Christians. Any idea of "natural law" or that this universe is a "fortuitous concourse of atoms" was not in the minds of the people they dealt with. Seldom did Jesus ask people to agree to propositions about God. That meaning of belief seldom played a part in the teachings of Jesus.

However, it does matter what we believe about God and about Jesus. A bishop in the seventeenth century wrote a book with the title *De Paucitate Credendorum*—"On the fewness of things that must be believed." You can make a good case for such a thesis; but whether the list be brief or long, it does matter—and it matters much—what you and I believe.

If we examine the Apostles' Creed we may be disappointed that it does not give a complete description of Jesus and of the Christian faith. It fails to mention Jesus' character, his teaching, his influence, his church, his inspiring example, his atoning death. When one learns, however, that the earliest form of the creed came from the second century, that it was used as the Christian profession of faith at baptism, and that it was designed to withstand and to be a bulwark against Gnosticism, we can appreciate it as a valuable help. Gnosticism taught that evil was identified with matter. Hence, the supreme deity of God could not come in contact with this present evil world and Jesus could not be both God and man. Thus viewed, the Apostles' Creed was not a summary of all Christian belief, but its central aim was to reject the Gnostic attack that Jesus was not both God and man.

Of all the many criticisms raised against Jesus, the evidence is most lucid, as even a questioner like Dr. Paul Tillich recognizes, that (1) Jesus maintained an unbroken unity with God, and (2) Jesus completely renounced every attempt to gain any advantage from this unity for himself.

Jesus endorsed the first of the great commandments, one which included loving God with the mind. This, then, does not grant an intellectual liberty to believe anything or nothing. We should, as "believers," study, analyze, and probe. We must dare to sift through and think out our beliefs carefully so that we know what we believe and why we believe it. A theology without religion is of small value; but a religion without a theology may not be any better.

There is a story of a fellow who went to his doctor saying, "If there's anything wrong with me, don't scare me by giving it a complicated, scientific, medical name. Just tell me in plain English."

"Well, to be frank," said the doctor, "you're just lazy."

"Thanks," sighed the man. "Now give me a scientific name for it so I can go home and tell my wife."

The name, the title, the creed is not the final value. You can believe a statement or a proposition *about* a person, but that is insufficient.

You can believe *in* a person, and that's the other side of the coin. Those who became believers not only held to certain ideas; they committed themselves to Jesus as a person and trusted in him. There is no Greek word for "faith" in this sense. When these new converts were called believers, they were being labeled as those whose trust led to discipleship.

Dean Wickes, of Princeton University Chapel, used to say that the greatest moment in a young person's life was not when he or she said, "I see the truth," or "That truth belongs to me," but rather, "I belong to it," or "Henceforth I am the servant of a great idea, a grand insight." This is the greatest moment in our lives, for henceforth we become mastered by this new and all-demanding relationship.

We may have certain opinions about a doctor, a lawyer, a senator, a president, or a minister, but the time comes when the real test is whether or not we dare to trust in that person, to confide in him or her, to really have faith in his or her integrity and goodness.

In the days when many moved to California, there was the story of an Easterner, recently arrived, who discovered that one of his neighbors was a charming eight-year-old girl. At every opportunity on the way to the office or on the way back, he would talk to her. One day he stopped for a longer time and found that she was not a member of his own denomination. She asked him, "What do they preach about in your church?" He answered, "Well, they preach the best they know."

The little girl then asked, "What is the best you know?" Being an experienced teacher, the man turned the question back to the child, "Well, what is the best that you know?" She thought for a moment or two, looked at him and answered, "The best I know is to have a friend."

The best I know is to have *the* friend, the Savior, in whom I trust and with whom I walk from day to day.

This is no fatuous, silly, saccharine plea for sentiment, or for gushy sentimentality in the name of religion. Naked imagination did something terrible to medieval Catholicism, and a spineless, nerveless sentiment can do the same for Protestantism in this day. It's unreal. We find no sentiment by itself in the New Testament. Not even the woman's lavish outpouring of the alabaster box upon the body of Jesus. It was passion! Emotions dare not be born outside the womb of thought and reality. Unreality is worse than dishonesty in the name of religion. The kind of dangerous hypocrite, both in state and in church, is the man or woman, not of fraud but of pose, not of dark and insidious design, but of subtle egoism, guilty of an unrealistic facing of the facts of human experience.

Have we taken stock of what we believe about God, about Jesus, about the church? Have we been using our minds? Are our beliefs stronger, with a firmer support of reason than a year ago? Have we used the opportunities which were presented to us to grow in our understanding of the Christian faith? Or have we just accepted them, too lazy even to question them?

In our joys and sorrows, hopes and fears, gains and losses, have we reached through to a deeper understanding of what God can do for us? Or are we failing in our witness, through cowardice or unwillingness to face sacrifice? Have we robbed the fellowship of our church by our indifference? Have we withheld any service which we might have given?

A friend has told of a little girl who was asked to bring her birth certificate to school one day. Her mother wisely cautioned her about the important document and told her not to lose it. The child forgot; you guessed it—she did lose it. When she became aware of her loss, she started crying. When asked why she was crying, she answered, "I lost my excuse for being born!"

Have we lost our excuse for being born?

We have if we are afraid to believe!

4.

To Say "I Love You"

"**E**ach time my parents, now in their seventies, conclude a telephone call, they say, 'Remember—we love you.'" What this college professor said about the words of her parents can generate helpful thoughts on the power that resides in an honest and frequent saying, "I love you."

One of the few commercial advertisements that portray a valid ethic is that of a telephone company asking us to "reach out and touch someone." That is fairly easy to do and relatively inexpensive, yet tremendously rewarding to both the speaker and the hearer.

Why, then, are we hesitant, if not afraid, to utilize this simple, effective expression?

It may be because the word *love* itself has lost its New Testament connotation; because it has acquired many additional meanings which are more secular, humanistic, and even evil. Thus, there is a reticence to express love, lest others read into our words a romantic "affair," or a cheap, tawdry jesting which has no sincerity in it.

Such a fear of being misunderstood has its roots in Puritanism, which taught that the body was sinful. To touch another's body, to show affection at all outside and beyond the matrimonial relationship, would be fraught with contamination of morals. Fortunately, we realize, theologically, that the body is sacred, that it houses God's spirit. We believe that there is no sharp line of separation between the physical and the spiritual. So we need not be afraid of touching someone with a word of love—or with a physical touch of holy affection. When we are told/shown by another in this way that we are loved, we are strengthened in our inner selves and motivated to love others in the same way.

Years after I had left the classes of my English professor, Dr. Havilah Babcock, at the University of South Carolina, he wrote these words in my copy of his book, *My Health Is Better in November:* "Whom I have admired and loved for twenty years." Those words continue to shine into my daily life, reminding me that there was a man who believed in me—and who said it.

Alice Freeman Palmer, principal of Wellesley College, profoundly influenced countless young women before she died at the age of forty-seven. It has been said that she had the gift of picking some quality in a student, commending it, and helping the student to share that quality with other students. One graduate wrote, "Mrs. Palmer had a strange effect on me. When I saw her, I felt as if I could do things that I never dreamed of before. Even now, whenever I think of her, I have a sense of dignity in my life . . . I shouldn't care to go on in a world in which she hadn't been." Alice Palmer incarnated love, the love that was eager to believe the best about someone. That love encouraged and strengthened—and it always does.

Kind, friendly words of love not only help to pull the best from us, they also can affirm that God cares for us in a very personal manner. When I was a young man, I heard Muriel Lester speak in London. She was a woman from a wealthy home who chose to give her life in serving the needy in East London. She literally invested her life for the down-and-outs through ministries at Kingsley Hall. She espoused unpopular causes, and she had a close relationship with Mahatma Gandhi. Muriel Lester became one of my heroines. How well I remember jotting down some words she spoke: "When you awake in the morning, immediately greet God as unseen Presence close beside you. Remind yourself in that early moment that you belong to God, that God is interested in you, and that God knows your name." With that deep commitment she went into the slums to show her love. Her example can help us to a similar level of grand living, overcoming pride and arrogance, not thinking more highly of ourselves than we ought to think. A poster I saw recently said:

> The more loving I become,
> The closer I am to God.

One of the big troubles with many of us is that we have come to think that we just don't matter to anyone; that if we faded from this world tonight, no one would really care. But the cross reveals to us that someone does care! In Jesus' suffering love we see the extent to which God will go and how much God bears for us so that we may come to him. To God everyone matters—very much! And so, the awareness of being loved that much does something to us and in us.

To know that we are loved can become the strong motivation to go beyond the words of friendship and to translate love and friendship into deeds. An old Quaker, after hearing one neighbor speak with sobbing tears over the misfortune that had come to another, looked at him and asked, "Hast thou felt sorry for him in your pocketbook?" Speaking love with deeds is the companion of speaking love with words.

Dr. John McFerrin was General Bragg's chaplain in the Confederate Army. One chilly day in November he was walking over the battlefield of Chattanooga, with a Bible in his hand. He was reading to the dying soldiers as they lay bleeding on the field. He walked up to one wounded soldier and said, "Let me read to you."

"Oh, Chaplain," said the soldier, "I am so thirsty; I am so thirsty." Wise chaplain that he was, John McFerrin ran to the nearest water he could find. Pouring some in his hat, he carried it to the soldier, and lifted it to his head, pressing the water to his lips. "Now, brother, let me read to you."

"Oh, Chaplain, I am so cold!" The chaplain doffed his light

overcoat and put it around the wounded man, touching him as tenderly as a mother would have her babe. The soldier looked up into the face of McFerrin and said, "Now, Chaplain, if there is anything in that book that makes a rebel chaplain treat a yankee soldier this way, read it to me."

A word can heal, a gesture can reassure, a smile can lighten a heavy burden, a touch can bring warmth into a chill of loneliness. Such are simple deeds that speak the language of love.

Love has the power to unlock doors in our lives. Love has the power to lead us back to a life we may have once known. From the shadowed valleys of selfishness, out of the arid planes of dull existence, God calls us to love one another. And when we respond to God's love, we know love for ourselves and for others. St. John of the Cross said it ages ago: "When the evening of this life comes, we will be judged on love."

5.

To Be an Innovator

Reading in the first chapter of John's Gospel, "The Word became flesh and dwelt among us," I suddenly thought of the word *fresh*. Why shouldn't God become *fresh* in us? Didn't Jesus come in order to call us to live as God wants us to—and in a fresh way every day? And when there is a fresh indwelling, often it will be along some new way and unexplored path.

It is then that fear and risk-taking "lock horns" in a struggle that will bring either success or regret. Two examples:

Two sons of a bishop, Wilbur and Orville Wright, dared to experiment with an invention that they thought would enable them to fly. This daring undertaking at Kitty Hawk, North Carolina, in 1903 was not even covered by most newspapers, including *The New York Times*. No reporter was sent to write about the risk. What an error in judgment!

In 1934 when some women in San Antonio, Texas, requested their denomination create a daily devotional guide, the bureaucracy accepted the idea. The first issue of *The Upper Room* magazine was created and instantly became a success, later reaching around the world and being published in over forty languages. But, the denomination's publishing house declined to manage it, saying it would not sell and therefore would become a liability. Another error in judgment!

Quite often in the record of the church, the governing bodies have not dared to be innovators. Halford Luccock commented on the story in Acts 4:1-2 about the reaction of the priests and the captain of the temple to the teachings of Peter and John: "Here was the officialdom of Jerusalem, 'sore troubled' at the advent of a new teaching. Officialdom spends a good deal of its time in a jitter. It easily gets sore troubled by any movement it does not itself start . . . officials as a group have learned to distrust ideas, except the petrified ones which form the basis of their authority."[1] This truth ought to become a constant warning and challenge to all who are entrusted with positions of leadership.

Take a look into the area of industry and economics. It is one thing to dare and to make discoveries and another to keep on experimenting with sales and distribution. Innovators in the United States of America invented the automobile, television, and computers. But Americans did not maintain the same efforts in how to manufacture and how to market these products. The Japanese became the discoverers of how to handle a wide distribution. Successful business means not only innovating the idea but also managing and selling the new idea. To be a leader in business is to have small room for satisfaction and contentment. To be an innovator is to respond to fresh undertakings.

"Thus says the Lord, stand by the roads, and look, and ask for the ancient paths" (Jer. 6:16, RSV). We should never discard the old ways which, having been tried, have been found to be helpful and productive. However, there is the ever-present temptation to enjoy the familiar, the ruts, so much that we turn aside from the call of the untried and unexplored. Lessons learned in using the old and familiar can be used in daring something new. How true this principle is in our personal living. Three suggestions:

1. Develop Self-discipline

In our prayer life we need to be on guard, lest the habit of regularity and sameness keep us from venturing into fresh ways, trying newly-worded phrases and modes of meditation. As fine as the Lord's Prayer is, I fear that many have taken it as a crutch and not as a ladder to new explorations. After all, Jesus gave the prayer as an example in response to the "vain repetitions" that "the heathen" were using in prayer. Often have I imagined that our Lord would add this petition, if he were teaching us today: "And grant us day by day some *fresh* discovery of your will." There is something fresh in putting such petitions into our communion with God. Seeking this kind of discipline can enable us to add stronger meanings to habitual phrases as we talk with others day by day.

—In thanking a cashier or filling station attendant, instead of merely saying, "Have a good day," try adding, "Have a good day—and night." You will be impressed by a keener response.

—In lieu of asking, "How *old* are you?" substitute this question, "How *young* are you?" Again, there will be surprise, if not shock, at this new version.

To be on the alert for fresh phrases calls for self-discipline, but what a joy there can be in making these discoveries.

2. Keep Hope Alive

The kind of hope that an innovator needs is that which expects something good to be found. (By contrast, *fear* is expecting something bad.) Hope believes in a future that will bring fulfillment of dreams.

In Bolivia years ago there was a young explorer seeking herbs and leaves, hoping to add to the storehouse of new medicines. Margaret Kreig discovered in the explorer's field notes what he had scribbled:

> I wonder what's around the bend?
> said the explorer.
>
> I wonder what that plant is?
> said the collector.

I wonder what's in it?
said the chemist.

I wonder what activity it has?
said the pharmacologist.

I wonder if it will work in this case?
said the physician.[2]

Today a daring venture is being carried out in the Andean mountains of Bolivia in an effort to bring basic health care to the Aymara Indians. The Andean Rural Health Project is pioneering to serve people who have had little in the way of health services since there is only one physician for approximately every 20,000 people.

The creator and director of the project is a young North Carolina doctor, Henry Perry III, whose academic training and medical experience at Duke and Johns Hopkins Universities have prepared him for this unique undertaking. He has believed that funds would be given. He has faced delays, "red tape," misunderstandings, conflicts. But all the while he has maintained a strong hope that the project would be blessed by God. Gradually, this hope is being translated into reaching the bodies and spirits of little children and older people in whose lives the spark of life was gradually dying. Other helpers have responded. This unusual venture under the banner of the Bolivian government's Health Ministry, the Bolivian Methodist Church, and Duke University went forward because hope was kept alive.

Some years ago plans called for a small village to be submerged where a lake was to be built. One day there came a visitor who was impressed by the run-down appearance of the houses and shops. When the residents were asked about the condition of the town, the answer came, "Why paint, why put on new roofs, when in a short time all will be washed away?" That night the visitor, depressed but observant, wrote this in his notebook: *Where there is no hope for the future there is no power for the present.*

3. Avoid Being Obsessed with Consequences

If Jesus had placed high priority on material values, it is doubtful that he would have gone to the cross. So it is in our efforts to create and explore and discover in the name of God. We simply cannot worry whether the price of our stock shares is rising or falling.

How refreshing to know a person who will give a daring, imaginative answer to a foolish question. There is a story from the life of Dr. W. B. Robertson of Scotland in the last century. One day he was approached by a member of a different denomination with these words:

> "I hear you are introducing some terrible innovations into your church service."
> "Indeed—and to what do you refer?" he asked.
> "I hear that you read the Ten Commandments at the Holy Communion."
> "Is that all you hear? We've introduced a far greater innovation than that."
> "What's that?" asked the lady, in some alarm.
> "We try to keep them," he said, with a twinkle.[3]

Spurning the results in dealing frankly with silly, foolish persons belongs to the committed and resolute Christian.

Afraid to become an innovator in our spiritual pilgrimage? Let's hope that each of us can experience *fresh* understanding and power as we ponder the significance of these lines—

Living depends on *loving*.

Loving depends on *knowing*.

Knowing depends on *risking*.

6.

To Speak Out

Why? Why are many of us afraid to speak what we believe? Usually we are not hesitant at all to voice our convictions about politics and business. Why do we have difficulty talking about our religious convictions? Is it because we fear the public reaction or the possible resentment of our peers? Is it because we are unsure and uncertain?

Could it be because of an opinion by a man, who, when asked to share his faith with a non-Christian, responded, "I will not witness because Jesus said 'tell no man'"? That reference invites a comment. More than once Jesus did give such counsel. After healing a leper (Matt. 8:4) and after Peter had declared his belief in Jesus' lordship, "[Jesus] charged the disciples to tell no one that he was the Christ" (Matt. 16:20, RSV). Most likely Jesus did not want those events recounted too quickly, with all emotion and no adequate reflection.

However, there is the other side of Jesus' teachings and actions. He sent them out, two by two, to tell what they knew. Matthew (28:19) records that after Jesus' resurrection, he gave a commission, "Go . . . and teach all nations." Before his ascension came these final words, "You shall be my witnesses" (Acts 1:8, RSV).

Why should a believer declare what Jesus means to him or her?

One reason lies in the *very nature of all religion*. Jesus wrote no books. He listed no detailed code of theology. He simply trusted the extension and spread of what he had revealed to the immediate disciples and to those in future generations who would believe. To think that religion can exist without declarations and witnesses is absurd. We proclaim because it is a logical result of our believing.

Another reason is closely related. *The world needs to know.* When there are teachers, preachers, lay witnesses who are willing to speak out, others will hear. Everywhere I have ever lived or visited there have been persons who needed to discover the joys and fulfillment found in a Christlike life. Their failures and fears clearly showed the need for a different way.

Our words, spoken or written, can be influential. In a church paper was an editorial on how basketball schedules were affecting church attendance. President William Friday of The University of North Carolina read the article and later telephoned the editor that he and his staff had rethought the matter and would not schedule any of their games on Sundays prior to 1:00 P.M. Others can be led by gentle persuasion to alter their habits and make new directions. Shared convictions can be influential.

No one should be afraid to speak out *when the word is authentic.*

In the days of Jeremiah, King Zedekiah asked the prophet, "Is there any word from the Lord?" When our words are clearly a real, authentic message from God, we can share them without any apprehension. When there is understanding by way of reason, tradition, and experience, it will be impressive, without a tinge of the make-believe or the counterfeit. Today we tend to make things look like something else. Counterfeit appearances in a religious sharing will not be worthy of our best.

When Jesus was questioned by Pilate, he responded, "Do you say this of your own accord, or did others say it to you about me?" (John 18:34, RSV). Is our message from our own being, or is it secondhand? Only the real thing will enable us to witness without fear. Unless what we have heard from others, even from the Bible itself, goes through our own being, mind and spirit, it will carry little effect.

During World War I, the famous British chaplain, G. A.

Studdert-Kennedy, said that God came ahead of the British Empire, and Downing Street politicians objected, saying the chaplain was disloyal to the king. This was his incisive reply: "I've been accused of being disloyal to the king. I don't know about that. What I do know is that I am loyal to Jesus Christ. If that isn't the same thing as being loyal to the king, then that's something for the king to worry about, not Studdert-Kennedy." Authenticity is stamped all across that kind of declaration.

The times are dangerous because we pervert the gospel by concluding that one's chief purpose is to be comfortable. Possessing peace of mind, we undercut the growth of courage in some dark hour of danger. Many times in the New Testament we find that when burdens were borne, wrongs were righted, and evils attacked, persons experienced strength of soul. Paul lived in the midst of danger, but fear was conquered by his faith in the living Christ, filling his thoughts with "whatever is true, whatever is honorable . . . just . . . pure . . . lovely . . . and gracious" (Phil. 4:8, RSV). Thus, there was little room for anxieties and fears.

On May 17, 1954, the United States Supreme Court announced its tremendous decision that segregation by race in public schools was unconstitutional. On the following Sunday in Main Street Methodist Church in Gastonia, North Carolina, where I was the minister, I gave my witness which was carried on television:

> My heritage is rooted in South Carolina. My own father owned slaves for a few years during the War Between the States and fought as a sixteen-year-old soldier in the last days. He lived through the hard days of reconstruction and adjusted himself to changed economic conditions and different race relations.
>
> For several years I have held the conviction that the practice of segregation cannot be defended on the basis of the Christian religion. For me, the Fatherhood of God, the Brotherhood of man, and doing unto others as you would have them do unto you do not sanction it.
>
> I live in and believe in a democracy, which includes the

executive, the legislative, and the judicial. Now that the highest judicial body in our Republic, consisting of nine men, appointed by three different presidents of the United States, has given this unanimous decision, I feel it my conscientious duty to do my best to implement this action helpfully, lovingly, patiently, and realistically.

My suggestions: First, let us face this decision as men and women of faith and courage! Let us believe in a God who loves us, everyone, and who has promised to go with us through all the varying currents of human experience.

Next, we should understand that every step cannot be taken at once; we need not try to cross all the bridges ahead. Let's face each one calmly and unafraid, remembering that as southerners and as Americans we have solved many major problems heretofore, and that today we are stronger than ever. Beware of what you say to your children and how you influence them, for they will live longest under these new conditions. Let us not prejudice their minds. There will continue to be the urgent importance of social limitations, both by the Whites and by the Negroes. We shall continue to choose our friends according to high concepts of ethics and morals.

May we resolve to keep our heads cool and our hearts warm with the love of God, knowing that we shall be able to find the right solutions as we go forth into this new world.

Anonymous calls and letters came. Threats were made with words so profane and filthy that I will not even list them. But the stance had to be made. A Christian dare not remain silent in such an hour.

When there is danger to human lives, there is urgent need to speak out. Dr. William Anlyan, Chancellor for Health Affairs in the Duke University Medical Center, recently reported that the largest number of illnesses treated in the Duke Hospital were first, from alcohol; next, from smoking; and third, from diet—too much salt and, or, too much sugar. If these habits are shortening the span of life, aren't they medically wrong? For some of us they are morally wrong. Therefore, it becomes the God-given responsibility for doctors to join ministers, journalists, and others in saying so, in speaking out, even in proclaiming the sin of losing life by what we eat and drink.

A discouraging fact about some church people is the hesitancy to take strong stands on crucial issues. Such reticence exists in lives of church leaders, clergy and laypersons as well. Too many Christians avoid controversial subjects or decline to take stands for the rights of minorities. Over the last fifty years, with only a few exceptions, the majority of those elected bishop in a Methodist denomination, before being elected, avoided controversial subjects or declined to take stands for the rights of minorities. If the church is not to become weaker in the days ahead, we who are called Christians must dare to speak out against nuclear war, racial injustice, dishonesty in public office, and any other actions of humanity that are in conflict with God's laws.

Let there be some "word from the Lord"! Let that word have Christ in the center. Even a quick and cursory examination of strong and fearless men and women will confirm the truth that they knew and experienced the companionship of the Master. The Book of Acts portrays the boldness of Peter and John, of Stephen, of Paul and of Barnabas. Their listeners "took note that they had been with Jesus." There is no other sure antidote to being afraid. We must let Christ be the center of our being, the author of our words and actions.

7.

To Face the Cross

The crucifixion makes some of us uncomfortable. Good Friday services are often not well attended. But because the cross deals with suffering and death is not enough to keep us from facing it. Nor is there reason enough in our delight with comfort and our preference for the niceties of affluent living.

Some say that because Jesus went to the cross, giving his life for all and thereby settling it once for all time, we need not be concerned. Then suddenly we remember his words, "Whosoever will come after me, let him deny himself and take up his cross, and follow me" (Mark 8:34, KJV).

If and when we do dare to face the cross, it has to be our choice, our deliberate decision, just as Jesus "steadfastly set his face to go to Jerusalem" (Luke 9:51, KJV). He knew what awaited him, but he did not turn back. So it will be with twentieth-century followers as our decision leads us to—*God, not self, at the center.*

In the garden of Gethsemane Jesus prayed, "Not what I want, but what you want" (Mark 14:36, TEV). Unless we can replace our self-centeredness—where our life rotates upon itself—with the centrality of God, then evil will control us. In Jesus we see a supremely joyous being because the only life fully without fear is God-centered. For Jesus there was no evasion of pain or sorrow or escape from crucifixion. And thereby came his uninhibited joy on his way to die: "These things I have spoken to you, that my joy may be in you, and that your joy may be full" (John 15:11, RSV).

When we face the cross, we have to deal with the question of "image." The image of self confronts us. Many who serve in public offices, including presidents of the United States, become intensely concerned over their image—"what are people thinking about me?" And this concern may take precedence over something more important, as a writer in *The New Yorker* points out:

> What most citizens fear is in peril when they contemplate the question of war and peace these days is the existence of mankind itself, but in the minds of certain public-relations experts in high places this vast dread concerning the life and death of all human beings has been supplanted by a certain nervousness concerning the mere image of one man.[1]

Visitors to Edinburgh, Scotland, can see many interesting places, but there are two which are especially memorable. One is the imposing memorial to Sir Walter Scott. Its centrality and uniqueness remind us of how this man faced what he hoped to avoid, yet did not lose heart. Such spiritual strength still illuminates our way to the cross.

Also in Edinburgh is one of the houses where Robert Louis Stevenson lived. Many are the mementos of his greatness. Always he was full of good cheer! His voice failing him, coughing up blood, and realizing death was always near, Stevenson continued writing grand stories and poetry. Once G. Ray Jordan said that there is nothing more important, more necessary, than for us to face life as Christ faced it. But we can do this only when we have in our minds and hearts the same divine spirit that swept him to victory, even on Calvary!

To face the cross without fear *we become involved*. In the description of the Great Judgment (Matt. 25:31-46), the only question put to us will be, did we feed the hungry, visit the prisoner and clothe the naked? Did we work to replace cruelty and injustice with kindness and justice? Any valid and helpful understanding of what the cross ought to mean will lie centrally in our willingness to become participants in the betterment of all persons.

We learn who Christ really is by ministering to needy and distressed brothers and sisters. The religious leaders of Jesus' day were surprised and amazed that this new Teacher identified himself with the poor and downtrodden. We should not be surprised when we hear the calls from little children dying because of no food and at that moment hearing the disturbing words, "As you did it not to one of the least of these, you did it not to me" (Matt. 25:45, RSV).

Howard Williams said it well in *Noughts and Crosses:*

> Jean Paul Sartre has shown us another way of looking at people. People who limit your lives, people who expose and humiliate you. People who are a nuisance and cause discomfort by their very presence. "Hell," says a character in one of his plays, "that is other people." Those who keep nagging us with their poverty and pleadings just when we have found security and prosperity. The people with empty mouths and aching hearts— Oh! that we could be rid of them and forget all about them. "Hell is other people" . . . but listen . . . for the Christian other people are Christ.[2]

This will mean some measure of suffering, some radical rearrangement of our values and priorities. When I am tempted to be unconcerned, it may take something strong, even radical, to cut away my complacency. One day I gave to a friend a small pocket cross, made of aluminum. On it was inscribed, "Jesus Christ is Lord." It was similar to one I carried in my pocket with my coins. Months later he said to me, "Remember that little cross you gave to me? It started cutting a hole in my pocket. So I filed down the corners so it would be smooth and not cut my pocket." That's it— how we try to smooth away the cutting power of the cross! Instead, we need to face what the cross is saying and asking: Get involved in the pain and agony of suffering persons.

I have read that a few days after the fall of Berlin, an American chaplain visited the underground apartments in Hitler's bunker. Things were exactly as Hitler had left them. In the study he was joined by a Russian who said he was an Orthodox priest. They gazed at a great portrait of Hitler, more than life-size, painted by one of the greatest artists of Hitler's Europe. They looked for a long time. The American turned away and idly examined some small articles on a little shelf. Among these he found a tiny miniature of the head of Christ. He showed it to the Russian who, after a long pause, looked around the bunker and said, "This is what happens when man is big and God is small."[3] Yes, when God is in the center, harmony instead of violence, gentleness instead of cruelty, love instead of hate becomes the dominant power in what we do.

The cross of Jesus stands in human history as the ultimate symbol of pain and injustice, and as such it stands by itself. However, in that cross is the eternal promise that earth has no experience that Christ has not shared. It rises as the apex of a triangle which subtends all lesser griefs and pains which humans can ever suffer. Therefore, when anyone takes a firm place along the base line he or she will discover the limitless promise of the crucified Lord, "I, when I am lifted up from the earth, will draw all . . . unto me" (John 12:32, RSV).

In the life of Paul, it is recorded that as he faced his ultimate cross in Rome, after friends greeted him on the edge of the city, "he gave thanks to God and took courage" (Acts 28:15, RSV). In giving our thanks for having a part in bearing our cross, we can share in the power of Christ which undergirds us and enables us to carry on. Whether or not it comes in our day, we can believe that we will share in the ultimate and final victory which the cross of Christ has won.

But stop! Heed the warning that when we walk the way of the cross there must be a lasting commitment. It is most apparent in the following story:

Clarence Jordan was a twentieth-century spiritual giant. He was a social prophet, the translator of the *New Testament in the Cotton Patch Version*, an organizer of the Koinonia Farm in Georgia. This last venture brought persecution, ostracism, and danger.

> In the early fifties, it is told, Clarence approached his brother Robert Jordan, later a state senator and justice of the Georgia Supreme Court, asking him to represent Koinonia Farm legally.
>
> "Clarence, I can't do that. You know my political aspirations. Why, if I represented you, I might lose my job, my house, everything I've got."
>
> "*We* might lose everything too, Bob."
>
> "It's different for you."
>
> "Why is it different? I remember, it seems to me, that you and I joined the church the same Sunday, as boys. I expect when we came forward the preacher asked me about the same question he did you. He asked me, 'Do you accept Jesus as your Lord and Savior' and I said, 'Yes.' What did you say?"
>
> "I follow Jesus, Clarence, up to a point."
>
> "Could that point by any chance be—the cross?"
>
> "That's right. I follow him to the cross, but not *on* the cross. I'm not getting myself crucified."
>
> "Then I don't believe you're a disciple. You're an admirer of Jesus, but not a disciple of his. I think you ought to go back to the church you belong to, and tell them you're an admirer, not a disciple."[4]

Am I only an admirer of Jesus Christ? A faith that is truly centered around the person of Christ will cause us, in looking *up* to the cross on which Jesus died, also cause us to look *in* our own hearts, to look *down* where there is evil and sin, to look *out* across the days to come, and thereby discover anew that the way of the cross does lead home to God.

8.

To Be Alone

If someone asked, "Name one of the characteristic marks of the twentieth century," how would you respond? I would surely note the awareness of living in a "social" world. We have been taught and directed by laws and bombarded by books and television to realize that we belong to groups.

This is a needed reaction to the self-centeredness and isolation that were largely prevalent in the nineteenth century. Many men especially had grown up under the delusion that they were self-made, giving little credit to others for their success and wealth. Rightly we have come to believe in social justice, in civil as well as property rights.

Entwined in much of contemporary living is the "hurry up" tempo. In our jobs there are quotas that must be done: a certain number of automobiles to be produced or a certain number of letters to be written in a given space of time. There is benefit in setting and holding goals; we should not discard them. But the danger comes when we let them get such a grip on our outlook that even in times of leisure we are controlled by a rigid work psychology. To prevent this grip from controlling us is the value of solitude, minutes to be alone in our thinking and responding.

This, then, is one of the dangers of our days—that we can fail to know both the need and the value in being alone. It is an awful danger when we fail to experience the joys of solitary moments. As an antidote there is rising a grand discovery of what moments of meditation can do for us. Spiritual formation, or devotional living, is producing not only a helpful dimension to a person's individual experiences, but it is spilling over into our churches and communities. The story of *The Upper Room*, with its worldwide outreach in the last fifty years has been properly titled, "A Twentieth Century Miracle." Why? Because we human beings have a need to be alone with God. And this need is being met as we are called to regular moments of prayerful thinking.

In the Bible those who stood tall spiritually at one time or another faced the struggle and the resultant benefits of being alone. Moses, while tending the flock of his father-in-law near the wilderness at the foot of Mr. Horeb, experienced the burning bush. It was while away from others that he received guidance and direction for his future role of leading God's people from slavery in Egypt (Exod. 3).

Elijah was another spiritual giant who found that one ought not to be afraid of facing God alone. Jezebel had threatened his life. He fled for safety, as most of us would have done. In despair he hid in a cave, only to have God question his actions. Responding to God, Elijah said, "I alone am left, and they seek to take my life" (1 Kings 19:10, NEB). Yet, it was then that he received his commission to return to the struggle. Earlier, when he was hungry, a messenger had urged him to eat, "lest the journey be too much for you" (1 Kings 19:8). It is safe to say that life's journey under any circumstances will be too much for us unless we pause in quiet to hear the voice of God.

Jesus, the Savior himself, before beginning his public ministry went into the desert. Deserts generally provide all the solitude one can handle. Again and again during his ministry, Jesus felt the urge to leave the crowds for purposes of heart-searching and renewal. If Jesus needed that kind of time alone, how much more do we need similar periods in the midst of turmoil, hurry, and strain!

We need not fear being alone because we need the *perspective* which can be gained from those times. We need to ask ourselves:

What is really happening to my sense of values? What is the biggest meaning in how I am living? Am I appreciating those with whom I work? Am I letting criticism and resentment get the best of my outlook? How to put all of these concerns into a healthy perspective becomes the yearning of our better selves!

There is a story of a weary, over-worked minister going to a skilled psychiatrist for help. "I'm working 14 hours a day, seldom at home with my family. I am whipped down." After a few questions, the minister was told to go and cancel all appointments for five days, write no sermons, and spend at least six hours each day quietly alone. After the third day, the psychiatrist was surprised by a visit from the minister.

"Why have you come so soon? Did you do as I told you?"

"No. I couldn't stand it. I make such bad company."

"Ah," said the psychiatrist, "now we see your problem. The very self you could not stand for even a brief time is the same self you have been inflicting upon others for 14 hours a day."

The *real* self comes to light when we dare to absent ourselves from the claims of others—not always, to be sure, but for intermittent periods when we discover the perspective of why we do what we do.

Persistence and *patience* are necessary. We dare not expect hasty and immediate results. Not sufficient are a few sessions of prayer during Lent. Albert Day wrote, "A minimum of a half hour of continuous concentration on God each day, and day after day, seems indispensable. And why not? We give many times that period of mental effort to projects that are 'dust and ashes' in comparison with the soul's quest for God."[1]

As I said in *Mark the Road:*

> [We have within us] a deep spiritual desire which cannot be satisfied merely by being community-minded or keeping busy with the machinery of religion at meetings and teas. We may go on saying, "Take your ease in days of affluence, eat, drink,

enjoy your popularity," but this simply shows we do not understand our nature. Yes, we will be frustrated, unhappy and chronically dissatisfied just as long as we suppress or ignore this inward hunger.[2]

The bottom line for spiritual growth, then, lies partially in turning away from being afraid to be alone. Truly it is in solitude that we hear those voices speak in the midst of our strife and disquiet, voices which haunt us in the busy street and office, that gently recall us when we go astray and awaken us when we idly sleep. "In the silences and solitudes, when alone, we meet ourselves and measure ourselves, not by the common standards of life in the presence of which we are so easily justified in proud sufficiency, but by those high and holy standards of God, the vision of which drives us to our knees with the cry, 'God be merciful to me, a sinner'. . . . Only as we face these intimacies does the soul grow and the secret of God become our own possession."[3]

Being willing to be alone brings a new and refreshing dimension to times of solitude. It can be a time when we honestly want to be in the near presence of our Lord. It can be a cleansing experience for us, with nothing in our hands to offer, with little or nothing to ask for, just being delighted to be in the presence of the Eternal. Then, the noiseless, quiet solitude of space and time can be transformed into a solitude of the spirit, even, of the heart. We then are prepared once again for the busy rounds of the everyday—and not afraid!

9.

To Handle What Happens to Us

So many things happen to us—the good and the bad, pleasant and unpleasant. "What has happened to me" was an apt and strong statement by Paul when he wrote to the Philippians. "I want you to know . . . that what has happened to me has, in effect, turned out to the advantage of the gospel" (Phil. 1:12, Phillips).

What in the world was Paul talking about? He was thinking about all of the difficulties and persecutions he had experienced; yet he had the audacity to say that these things have worked out to the advantage of the gospel and to the blessing of the work of God. He wrote these words from a prison cell, and herein is an index to something of far-reaching significance and power.

Good things and bad things happen to everybody. The writer of the Book of Ecclesiastes wrote, "All things come alike to all. There is one event to the righteous, and to the wicked" (Ecclesiastes 9:2, KJV). He recognized even then that marching armies do not make detours around the homes of the virtuous and honored. We know that disease germs invade the homes of the wicked as well as the faithful servants of the living God. We have wanted to believe that the universe is arranged especially for the suitability and convenience of righteous people. We say, tongue-in-cheek, when someone succeeds, "He must be living right." It is difficult to shake off the idea that a Christian should never be attacked by failure or by disease or be hurt by the hammer blows of life.

In the New Testament there is one clear word: In this world all of us will have tribulation. The word *tribulation* comes from the word *tribulum* which was a heavy stick on the end of a rope used by a farmer to beat down on the straw in order to separate the chaff from the good grain. The *tribulum* is a part of your life and mine.

For instance, two people stand before a large rock. One person carves a statue from the rock; the other person beats it to pieces. Two people turn to the same dictionary. From identical words one person writes something which leads people to turn toward God, while the other person uses the same words to write something that turns people away from God. Someone once gave this illustration: If you take a piece of wax, a piece of meat, a lump of clay, some wood shavings, and put them all on fire, the same degree of heat will, of course, affect them. But over the fire, the wax melts, the meat fries, the clay hardens, and the wood shavings burn up. That becomes a description of how the fires of life's tribulations bring one response from one person and a different response from another. Some of us grow weaker, and some of us grow stronger; some of us just fade away.

It was George Buttrick who first called my attention to a fact about the three crosses on Golgotha outside Jerusalem. On those crosses were three dying men. The wood of the crosses was the same, the nails were the same, the downward drawing of the blood was the same, and the same sun beamed down upon their bodies. One event—but look at the difference! One event drew from the man on the left a violent curse, from the man on the right a sudden penitence, and from the man in the middle, instead of resentment, the words, "Father, forgive them; for they know not what they do" (Luke 23:34, RSV).

It's a fact: A wind which blows over a stagnant cesspool carries disease; the same wind blowing over a flower garden carries wonderful fragrances. Water falling on molten metal makes it hard, but water falling on a wheat field makes it fertile. Sorrow makes one person rebellious and another person braver and more gentle. Death on the *Titanic* made men rush for lifeboats regardless of women and children, but there were two other men standing on the rail of that sinking boat as the lifeboats pulled away. One of them waved his hand and pointed to his dinner jacket, "If we must visit Neptune, it is better to go well dressed." The other man waved his hands saying, "Give my love to the folks back home." One disaster at sea, but what a difference in the responses!

It is possible for us to respond to the things which happen to us in a kind of *submissive* manner, which is basically the reaction of Stoicism. We accept what happens because we believe it to be inevitable. This is a kind of fatalism, and it is a part of some major religions. The word *Islam* means "submission." The Moslem Arab crossing the desert, finding an oasis to be dry, does not resent nor question that fact. He wraps his robe around him and passively waits for death. It is the inscrutable will of Allah.

Some Stoicism has crept into Christianity. We say we will keep a stiff upper lip and quote William Ernest Henley: "It matters not how straight the gate, how charged with punishments the scroll, I am the master of my fate: I am the captain of my soul." But this is not basic Christian doctrine. If this is all that Christians have, it is nothing more than a kind of "baptized fatalism." One of the great debates in the last century has been in the effort to clarify the meaning of God's will and the nature of humankind's obedience to it. We have come a long way from thinking that evil things—poverty, pestilence, disease, and ignorance—exist as visitations of the Almighty. We may admire people with a Stoic disposition, but it is not Christianity. Mere endurance is short of the positive redemptive principle to which the New Testament points.

Another response to the things which happen to us is one of *resentment*. We cry out, "Why does this happen to me?" Then we pity ourselves into a self-righteous dither. To continue this sort of response is the fertile ground for a real neurosis.

Many people never come to terms with simple reality—that life in this world is not designed to run smoothly. We have been fed on so much of Freudian ethics which someone has called "apathetic ethic" that we really have little, if any, philosophy for failure. Do you remember in the early days of the automobile when the tire manufacturers tried to produce a tire that would stand the shocks of the road? First, they tried to make one that was hard and tough so that it would resist the shocks, but they discovered that it was soon pounded to pieces. They came to learn that they had to make a tire which would give, which would absorb the shocks. That tire was enduring because it was resilient. It could expect the shocks and respond to them. It is something of the Christian spirit to move beyond resentment into a spirit of acceptance revealed in Paul's words quoted earlier for the Philippians.

The Christian approach is the more excellent way, and that is to respond, not resentfully or submissively, but *creatively*. Christian disciples walk so close to their Master that they see how the hard-to-take things are not misfortunes to be resisted or burdens to be passively resigned to, but rather are the things which are to be used creatively in building the temple of life.

Here is an intensively dynamic principle which we need to comprehend. Did you ever participate in the game called "running the gauntlet"? The idea is for two rows of boys to line up facing each other; each boy is armed with a switch or kind of stick which would not kill, but which would hurt. The fellow who was requested to run the gauntlet would drop down on all fours and as fast as he could he would run through that trap with sticks and switches coming down. No matter how fast he traveled, he always came out at the other end. However, he was either a *better* person or a *bitter* person. Life is not altogether unlike that. Things happen to us, and no one of us can truly be a mature adult until we have gone through the gauntlet and know that we have discovered some wisdom and some strength of soul which have come through the hammer blows.

There are some things which only trouble can bring out of a person. It was Beethoven who said of Rossini that he had in him the making of a great musician if he had only had some difficulties to struggle with and some failures. He wrote too easily and, thus, he never achieved greatness. Let me say this to all of us, young and old alike: we will never be much good until we have run the gauntlet; until we have learned to take creatively the things which happen to us and use them to the glory of God.

In reading the Gospels we can see the things which happened to Jesus. He experienced poverty. He experienced temptation. He suffered criticism. He was the victim of misunderstanding. He was betrayed by his closest friends and nailed to a cross. And, yet, Jesus was able to use that cross so that it has become the universal symbol of redemption and love.

One day a mother sent her son to buy twelve bananas. On the way home, he became hungry. The bananas tempted him, so he ate two of them and then told his mother that the money she had given him would buy only ten bananas. Months later he was at the movies and suddenly he recognized himself portrayed on the screen eating those two bananas as he walked down the street. A film company had been searching for local color and real-life situations and had taken shots of that street at the very moment the boy was eating the bananas. Yes, the conviction persists, but the picture is always taken in every home and on every street—even though our human eyes may never see it. What happens to us brings out what is in us. It does not so much matter what happens *to* you. What happens *in* you matters more than I can say.

It takes a large measure of willing trust, a continuing experience of praying "thy will be done," and a bravery of soul by way of trusting and praying if we are to say with Paul, "What has happened to me has, in effect, turned out to the advantage of the gospel."

10.

To Face Tomorrow

It has been said that our lives are like a diary in which we mean to write one story and write another. And our humblest hour is when we compare the volume as it is with what we promised to make it. This idea, more than the affidavit of some despairing, despondent soul, strikes home as one basic reason why many of us fail to reach the goals we have set for ourselves: We keep looking toward tomorrow and putting off until some later date the responsibilities and privileges which the present is throwing at us.

A young man, squeamish and hesitant, wrote to his girl the following lines: "Darling, I love you with all my heart. Nothing in the whole world will ever keep us apart!" And then he added a postscript: "I'll be over to see you tonight if it doesn't rain." This last phrase aptly describes so many of us with good intentions. We pretend and we profess—but we slip into the habit of letting some little inconvenience stand between us and the realization of those purposes. Edward Young was eternally correct when he wrote in "Night Thoughts":

> Procrastination is the thief of time;
> Year after year it steals, till all are fled,
> And to the mercies of a moment leaves
> The vast concerns of an eternal scene.

In Acts 24 there is the record of a man who committed the

colossal blunder of putting off the acceptance of Jesus Christ when that opportunity was given to him by Paul, the missionary. So far as the Bible tells us, Felix never did get around to a convenient time for affirming his discipleship of Jesus. And therein lies the paramount danger—we put off and keep on putting off until it is too late!

Felix said, "Go away for the present" (Acts 24:25, RSV). He thought that he could separate himself from Paul—that he could get rid of him. It seems to be human nature to want to get rid of someone who would disturb us, someone who would remind us of our faults and failures. We want to say, "Go on! Get out of my way! Mind your own business!" But it is one of life's most fundamental laws that we cannot separate our lives from others. We may establish a separation for a short duration, but in the long run we are all bound together. We share some sort of influence with our family, with our neighbors; our road leads into some other road and forms a crossroads. We come face to face with others. This mighty truth is revealed in the story of Esther in the Old Testament. Mordecai was showing this young Jewish girl that she could not escape from her responsibility by being in the seclusion of the king's palace. Mordecai challenged Esther with these words: "Who knows whether you have not come to the kingdom for such a time as this?" (Est. 4:14, RSV). She had an opportunity and therefore an obligation—the two always go together. Every opportunity carries a definite obligation!

"None of us lives to himself, and none of us dies to himself," Paul declares in his letter to the Romans (14:7, RSV). We have the responsibility of influence. I firmly believe that God does and will hold each of us responsible, not only for our individual deeds but also for the influence which we exert upon some other person or upon some group of people.

Once there was a young missionary who worked among non-Christian natives. They found it difficult to learn to read the Gospels. One day one of the natives was asked what it meant to be a

Christian, and he quickly answered, "It is to live like Mr. Wray." This person had learned from the life of Mr. Wray, the missionary, the very likeness of Jesus Christ. Although he could not read Matthew, Mark, Luke, or John, he was reading the life of this young Christian missionary. Our influence is powerful.

Felix said, "Go away *for the present*"—and thereby yielded to the fallacy of thinking that just this one time would not matter. Evidently he thought that he would have plenty of time to consider this question of religion. This is one of the most certain laws of human experience: Every time we procrastinate makes it even more difficult to take the right step the next time.

"When I have an opportunity I will summon you" (Acts 24:25, RSV). That sounds so modern, so very contemporary to our ears. We ourselves have spoken it frequently, and we have heard others say it. A pastor hears it often: "Well, I am not ready to join the church yet. I am not good enough (I want to sin a little while longer). There is plenty of time to change." And there are those church members who have grown cold and indifferent to the appeal of God and to the voice of conscience. It is just not convenient this Sunday to go to Sunday school and to the worship services. They will go next Sunday, and lo and behold when next Sunday rolls around, they find it even more difficult to get up and go to God's house. In fact, that "opportunity" actually never does come. We have to rise above our feelings, beyond our moods, and act upon duty and that which is right and that which God requires of every disciple.

"I'll be happy when" is a popular rationalization:

- I'll be happy when I get out of school.
- I'll be happy when we have a baby.
- I'll be happy when I make a certain salary.
- I'll be happy when all of our bills are paid.
- I'll be happy when we move into our new house.

All of that is delusion. The simple truth is that the time for happiness is today, not tomorrow!

See how this temptation works in everyday life. Haven't you put your work off until at last it has to be done in a hurry, often in a very shoddy and poor manner? The growth of our spiritual lives also is held back by this habit of procrastination. Who has not neglected praying at times because it was not convenient to pray?

We also postpone caring for our loved ones. Sir John Squire wrote some lines in which he depicted a man who persistently neglected a loved one. He had intended again and again to write the loved one a letter. But there was always the demand of business, and he has kept putting off writing. "Tomorrow I will do it," he told himself. "Certainly I will write tomorrow." But the letter was never written. Then one day a message came. He tore the sealed envelope open. His loved one had died. As the man stood there, staring at the death message, remorse rushed in like a flood. "It shall not be today," he cried. "It shall not. It is still yesterday. There is time still—there must be time." Poor, unhappy man. He learned that soon there will be time only for regret. Time is passing on. The years add up quickly and soon our chances are forever gone. An unknown author wrote these lines:

> He was going to be all a mortal should be tomorrow;
> No one should be braver or kinder than he tomorrow,
> A friend who was troubled and weary he knew,
> Who'd be glad of a lift and who needed it, too;
> On him he would call and see what he could do, tomorrow.
>
> Each morning he stacked up the letters he'd write tomorrow,
> And thought of the folks he'd fill with delight, tomorrow,
> It was too bad, indeed, he was busy today
> And hadn't a minute to stop on his way;
> More time he would have to give to others, he'd say,
>   tomorrow.
>
> The greatest of workers this man would have been,
>   tomorrow;
> The world would have known him had he ever seen
>   tomorrow,

But the fact is he died and faded from view,
And all that he left here when living was through
Was a mountain of things that he intended to do—tomorrow.

An old fable, so Harry Wilkinson tells us, describes "a horse who ran away one morning from its stable and didn't return until the evening. When his master upbraided him, the horse said, 'But here I am safe and sound. You have your horse back. Why worry?' 'True,' replied the master, 'but my field is unploughed.' "[1] There it is; the unploughed fields will forever rebuke us if we yield over and over to this matter of postponing and putting off. God has work to be done—right now, in your community, in your home, in your church. Time is not waiting. It is high time to destroy selfishness and to give time and energy for the cause of saving human life.

John Greenleaf Whittier, one of the gentlest souls who ever lived, warns in "The Answer" that because of delay we may ultimately lose all desire and power to make the right decisions:

> Forever round the Mercy-seat
> The guiding lights of Love shall burn;
> But what if, habit-bound, thy feet
> Shall lack the will to turn?
>
> What if thine eye refuse to see,
> Thine ear of Heaven's free welcome fail,
> And thou a willing captive be,
> Thyself thy own dark jail?

Many years ago, Dr. J. H. Jowett was speaking to a group of undergraduate college students on the brevity of time: "I find it set down in tables that the average duration of human life at the age of twenty-one is thirty-six years. We may hope for a little more, we may fear a little less, but speaking generally a period of thirty-six years, or about 13,000 days, is the term in which our tasks must be accomplished." Our life expectancy has been lengthened a little, but the truth is still there. We dare not postpone life's spiritual issue, fraught with the significance of eternity, until a tomorrow which may never come! Tomorrow is not ours to fear if we claim this moment, this day!

Ours is the privilege to reassess our confidence in God, not only of yesterday and today, but also of tomorrow. On many sides come wailings and woes that humankind is about to become extinct. I do not believe that to be true. To be certain, likely there will be killings and violence—but not extinction! The creator God has put too much into this planet upon which we reside to let it end in a bang. God gave Jesus Christ for our redemption. God will not let the ones for whom Jesus gave his life go down the drain. Some may argue the theology of this affirmation, but it is more than blind determinism.

It is vital faith in both the wisdom and goodness of God which supports and undergirds our freedom of choice. Such freedom does not outrun or supersede the nature of God!

Praise God for being vitally alive *today*! Praise God for the assurance that God will be present with us in all of the tomorrows!

11.

To Be a Dreamer

On his first visit to London, a young minister saw a theater marquee advertising a play. He did not go in to see the drama, but the name of the play enriched his life through the years that followed: *Wake Up, Then Dream*. Through the centuries of record-ed thought, dreams have attracted our interest and study. In the twentieth century, psychologists such as Freud and Jung have advanced interesting theories, but none of them·are really satisfy-ing. Our dreams during hours of sleep rightly do concern us. As far back as the days of Joseph this was true. One morning when Joseph saw his fellow-prisoners—the butcher and the baker—looking disconsolate, he asked, "Why do you look so sad?" They replied, "We have had dreams, and there is no one to interpret them" (Gen. 40:8, RSV).

We learn not to be afraid of dreams by *willingly dedicating our subconscious to the guidance of the Holy Spirit*. What goes into a dream is in some way, although not rationally explained, a part of our being. Surely it is both false psychology and false theology to split a person into several parts and suppose that one is redeemed and the other not. Certainly Jesus did not come to save only the conscious or the body. Each of us is a very mysterious combination of the spirit and the body, of matter and mind, and redemption deals with the whole being.

So, we may put a nighttime dream to good use. If a dream was disturbing, the next morning it is wise to talk about it in our prayers.

It has been a part of our night and it ought to be shared, consciously and purposefully with God. In this manner whatever harm or fear or alarm may have surfaced it can be redeemed by our dedicating it directly to God. What if the dream was good, helpful and enjoyable? It, too, can and ought to be shared in our moments of meditation. The joyful belongs to God as much as the sad and despairing. When we include our joyful dreams we move in the direction of making them more and more a part of our conscious and willful being. Likewise, by praying over the bad dream we can remove the undesirable from our intentional being.

The body is a part that rightly belongs to God; the spirit is a part that belongs to our Maker. A story has been told of a clergyman and a sailor being very sick in adjacent beds of a hospital. They both became delirious, or simply "talked in their sleep." The clergyman swore violently, and the sailor prayed fervently. Yes, the whole of us—our affinities with the material in which we spend a few years of mortal experience—and our affinities with the eternal beyond space and time. All of this we should dedicate to the guidance of the Holy Spirit.

The fact that often we are helpless in getting an interpretation of thoughts of the subconscious is not nearly as interesting and as challenging as the kind of dreams which we come to have when we are wide awake. When we are awake, *we can purposefully dream.*

It has long been a maxim that in both young and old there is power in having a vision; "Your old men shall dream dreams, and your young men shall see visions" goes back to the days of Joel (2:28, RSV). Aimlessness has plagued the lives of many people in each generation. Winston Churchill, a man possessed with dedicated purposes, was once asked why many people of his own age had failed in business and professional life. "Because they had no clear-cut goals" was reportedly his telling reply. Behind many suicides there has probably been more the lack of a clearly defined *purpose* for living than simply *failure* in achieving. The difference it makes is often revealed in the effect upon physical health.

Years ago a former city editor in New York was convicted of a crime and sentenced to prison. He became ill and was put in the prison hospital. The warden sought to challenge him.

"Charlie," he asked, "how would you like to get out of bed?" Chapin—that was his name—shook his head.

"I think I'll put you to work, Charlie," continued the warden. But the man's brows contracted in a frown and again his head signaled, "No."

"Something that I think you will like," suggested the warden. "You will be the editor of the *Bulletin*."

"The *Bulletin* was then the prison paper. A rather haphazard publication, it needed somebody to make it. Chapin seemed to understand. His eyes bored into those of Lawes, who added, "But you will have to get well in quick order, otherwise the offer is withdrawn. We can't wait too long." The new editor was out of bed in a week.[1]

For many, the plays of Eugene O'Neill are too heavy, even depressing, but I have discovered in many of them the nobility of dreams. Someone has quoted O'Neill as saying that a man cannot live without a dream, regardless of how shabby that dream may be. In O'Neill's play *A Touch of the Poet,* the leading character relives the time when he wore a resplendent military uniform and played out the role of a hero on the battlefield. That his dream was far removed from reality did not matter. In fact, the dream became reality in mind and spirit. It would seem that as long as we are alive, we are intended to follow a dream; for if the dream vanishes, there is little left worthy of our endeavors. The apostle Paul wrote, "I press on toward the goal . . ." (Phil. 3:14, RSV).

As the years of advancing age possess us, many of our earlier dreams are impossible. Our options are fewer. It is easy to become bitter and resentful. But other dreams, even though more modest and not as exciting, can possess us and add zest to daily experiences. Our souls feed on the stuff of high visions—not the fantasies of idle daydreaming, but the pull and tug of reaching for the doing of God's will through whatever talents we have—*by actively seeking to fulfill God's dream.*

A desire voiced by an unknown writer, "Let me be the self the Potter dreamed I'd be," confirms the conviction that *each one of us is a dream of God.* For every person brought into creation through the gate of birth, the divine Creator has a purpose and a plan. The training, teaching, and example of parents are potent influences for each of us. Yet we ourselves—our choices of direction—will be the ultimate factor in our realizing God's dream. This is exactly why the words of the unknown poet are so important:

> Let me have a faith
> that my tears demand of me.
>
> Let me grow a love
> that the world expects of me.
>
> Let me find a cause
> that pulls the best from me.

The first Christian sermon ever preached, so far as the record goes, was on the Day of Pentecost when Peter urged his hearers to be saved "from this crooked generation" (Acts 2:40, kjv). Peter was convinced that Jesus as Lord and guide would enable persons to find their purpose in the creative purposes of God. Across the intervening years one of the keenest and truest interpretations of salvation in Christ has been that we are enabled to let our words and deeds be under his direction.

William Barclay wrote that there are three essentials to a local church's becoming a power station—vision, work, and prayer. "To work to the limit of one's strength; to pray with all the intensity of one's being; to lift up one's eyes and to see the harvest to be reaped—these are the things which will make a congregation a real power house for Christ."[2]

If this be true of a group, how much more is it true of the individual who is consciously pointing towards fulfilling God's dream for him or her.

What can we do to fulfill God's purpose? First, some questions we can ask ourselves, honestly and directly, as we commune with God: "Will I deliberately try to achieve God's desire this day?" At night, we ask, "To what extent did I fulfill God's way today?" These frank inquiries of ourselves will go far in making our prayers truly alive and strengthening.

Second, as we pray, it can be helpful to make a list along these lines: 1. What can I *do* positively that will please God? Name specific persons and deeds that I know will be authentic and fulfilling. 2. What things will I guard against that I know to be unhealthy? Failure to control my temper, over-indulgence of my body, failure to respond to human need of a neighbor or those faraway, speaking evil about someone, etc. 3. What *changes* in my habits will I deliberately seek during the upcoming hours? Here again, the more specific we are, the more progress we will effect in spiritual growth.

These lines of spiritual achievement have proven effective in many lives. Here is an illustration. One morning, a minister's secretary announced, "A woman is here to see you. She says it is urgent." The woman introduced herself to the minister, saying, "I have never met you before. But last night I dialed the Dial-a-Prayer number and heard your recorded prayer. I was faced with a tremendous decision. My neglect of God and of the church had brought me to a crisis. But your prayer led me to choose the better way. Today I am so happy and free, and just wanted you to know it." What was that prayer?

> God, help me in the hours of this day and night to become the person that in my best moments I really want to be. Amen.

What we have been affirming is precisely that God speaks to us most powerfully when we are earnestly planning and working at becoming our best selves. Not content with pleasant worship times that fail to move out into deeds and acts, we shall believe that the finest call is the call to service. We shall pray to be delivered from idle and fruitless daydreaming. We shall pray that we may be led by the Holy Spirit, wherever we are and whatever the circumstances may be. We shall continue daily to be pulled by God's dream, knowing that a brighter and better tomorrow awaits.

Mother Teresa of Calcutta, truly one of God's grandest servants, is reported to have told Henri Nouwen: "If you spend one hour a day in contemplative prayer and never do anything which you know is wrong, you will be all right."[3] She probably did not intend that to be complete guidance, for in her own life she clearly demonstrates the power of being possessed by God's dream.

All of us stand in strong need of launching out in daring deeds on unknown and uncharted seas. Then—and only then—will we demonstrate the grandeur of dreaming—dreaming when we are wide awake!

12.

To Be Afraid

A friend of mine had spoken in an evening chapel service on a college campus. While walking away, he overheard a conversation between two coeds. One said, "He kept talking about sin, but what did he mean?" The other girl replied, "Oh, that has something to do with Adam and Eve."

It was only the word that puzzled these girls. If someone had stolen their new clothes, they would have known about the sin of stealing. If a man had been untrue to their affections, they would have known about the sin of unfaithfulness. The experience was real, but the word was without meaning.

During the war in Vietnam, I visited in Saigon, meeting with chaplains and other church leaders. At the airport as I prepared to leave, I placed my luggage to be checked. After presenting my ticket and passport, I glanced at the luggage and was shocked to see printed on the tags—SIN. Then I realized that this was the abbreviation of my next destination, Singapore.

That picture has been etched upon my memory, for surely as we travel in any day or night on the trip of life, we have with us the constant potential for sin. It is, therefore, quite natural to be afraid of yielding to sin.

It is easy to try evasion by using other names, such as, "infraction of social custom," or "juvenile shortcoming." We often blame our wrongdoing on the genes given to us by our parents or because of our peers or because of where we reside. Or, we laugh about our secret, hidden sins. D. L. Dykes makes the point by saying to a congregation, "If I announced that at the end of the service a nurse would be at the central aisle exit with a vaccination that would cure our most cherished sin, most of us would hurry out the side doors."

When we fear sin, we will not surrender to a feeble effort of evasion. "In the heart of every human being, whether he lives on Main Street, U.S.A., or in the jungle of the Amazon, there lurks a vague uneasiness, a sense of inner wrongness, and a built-in hunger for rightness. This is the badge of our creaturehood; uneasiness in the heart, sometimes called 'the sense of guilt.' And there is no use sweeping it under the rug or taking it to the seashore or the mountains in some Shangri-la of forgetfulness. The uneasiness is within."[1]

Being afraid of evil in the early stages of thought, before the deed is done, can be a spur to acting righteously. The New Testament affirms that "perfect love casts out fear" (1 John 4:18, RSV).

In love there is no place for fear. There is, however, a broad inclusion in love's dimension. Having the capability of being afraid is God-given; in it there is an *ultimate* goodness. When you have a toothache, it sends you to the dentist. Likewise, when there is the urge to evildoing, there is a legitimate fear. God has given us this capability so that we will be uneasy with our sins. If a wrong is closeted within, sooner or later an alarm bell goes off, saying, "You cannot do wrong and not be afraid." By this lucid criterion, we ought to thank God, realizing that this kind of fear can become our helper.

To look at the symptoms of some moral infection is not enough. To deal only with guilt feelings is not enough. What we must deal with is the guilt itself. This is exactly the trouble with many of us— we are not afraid of the deed, of the guilt.

The other side of the coin tells that we need not fear or be afraid of the solution. The cure is to be greeted and accepted.

What can we do about it? Can we cleanse ourselves? The answer lies in the power of God through Christ. Our willingness to be cured, to be forgiven is man's part—but only God can do the forgiving. Sin always contracts guilt. Suffering and damage are temporal, while sin is in its nature, eternal. Sin, when committed cannot be called back, we cannot forgive ourselves. These lines from "Rock of Ages" say it without equivocation:

> Could my tears forever flow,
> Could my zeal no respite know,
> These for sin could not atone.

God does not annul sin by fiat or dictatorial law—forgiveness is not like that. God does not say, "Forget it. I'll let you off easy this time if you promise not to do it again." But God does relieve us of guilt in the sense of loving us who have done the wrong, though not defending the wrong itself. God cannot take back the consequences of our acts, because God cannot retract the laws established in the very nature of things. When we go against the laws of life, we bring the inevitable results upon ourselves. God cannot take off the consequences and put them on another. Paul wrote that what we plant is what we will reap (see Gal. 6:7). But God does take the consequences with us, as if to say, "We will face this mess together to create a new consequence from the evil consequence." And I hasten to assure you that this is no easy-going doctrine, because the new consequence cannot be created until after we have suffered the bad results of our deeds. Søren Kierkegaard said, "Life can be understood backwards; but it must be lived forward." In a backward look we see that our own lives have been a series of partial successes and remade failures. We had to cooperate, but whenever we were made humble and contrite and obedient, our life was reshaped in unforeseen ways.

We are all sinners. Call it anything you desire, the truth abides: "All have sinned and fall short of the glory of God" (Rom. 3:23, RSV). The writer of First John said, "If we say we have no sin, we deceive ourselves, and the truth is not in us. If we confess our sins, he is faithful and just, and will forgive our sins and cleanse us from all unrighteousness" (1:8-9, RSV). Confession is necessary—always necessary—because there is no victory over a sin of which we are not conscious. This is the truest psychology of modern teaching as well as the heart of the Christian gospel. The old Methodist phrase "conviction of sin" stood for a vital truth. I must stand convicted in the court of my own mind before any salvation is possible. That personal conviction is naturally a confession of guilt. That is why I am saying that we had better look at sin as sin, face its reality, take off the coverings and thereby be ready to admit our confession. When confession is made to God and God has pardoned us, giving us that inner witness and inward assurance, then we are restored in fellowship with our Creator. We feel at one with God. We feel and we believe that we are in harmony with God's purposes for us and for the world.

Once I had a dream. The chairman of the parsonage committee called to say the committee wanted to make needed repairs on the parsonage and that a man would be out to see me. He came, and I pointed out the need of stopping leaks on the back porch, of fixing a screen door, and other such repairs. He indicated the work crew would be out the next day. And the next day came. I was in the upstairs study writing a sermon when I heard a noise, then louder noises, and then violent sounds which caused me to run to the stairway. I saw men with crowbars and axes tearing out the plaster and battering down a door.

"Wait," I shouted. "Something is wrong. This is not my house! Don't tear it down. What are you trying to do?"

"Oh, Mr. Weldon,'" said the foreman, "after looking around we decided that what this house needed was not a few repairs, but a complete rebuilding. And that's what we are going to do—a major remodeling."

And then I was awake. But what a message! We need not a little patching on our spiritual house, not a few moral adjustments, not the rubbing on of soothing ointment. We need to come to the Master for a complete renewing, asking forgiveness of our sins, and then living on a different and higher level. Whatever be our sins, we go to the Master Builder. Whether it be the wrong choice, whether it be selfishness, whether it be ignorance, whether it be social or individual evil, let's face it as such—as the breaking of God's will. No matter what the title or the name, it is sin. And only God can forgive sin. The old hymn by Thomas Moore points the way:

> Come, ye disconsolate, where'er ye languish,
> Come to the mercy seat, fervently kneel.
> Here bring your wounded hearts, here tell your anguish:
> Earth has no sorrow that heaven cannot heal.

In these pages we have pondered the wisdom of not being afraid. Is it now a contradiction to affirm that it is permissible and wise to be afraid of sin and its consequences? Certainly not! To have the "fear of the Lord" is to have a strong and vital trust in God's love and power to guide us *through* and *over* our wrongs. The courageous believer can rightly evidence his or her bravery in facing the sins that so easily beset us.

Epilogue

A multitude of fears confront us every day: sickness, financial loss, old age, criticism, loss of friends. Young people in particular fear failure in school examinations, sex, not getting a job, unpopularity, appearing naive.

I believe that fear is the archenemy of noble living. It stifles enterprise, saps endeavor, hides the sun from our view with thick clouds of doubt. It gives birth to dangers that do not exist. It curtains doors which are open and the paths that lead to the top of the hills.

Fear is the expectancy of the bad, while faith is the expectancy of the good. The choice of how to live, by fear or by faith, is ours each day that we experience the mixture of joy and sorrow, of triumph and failure.

> To be victors over life and not victims of it, really to keep heart and courage, we must have faith; faith that there is meaning to life, faith that it does eternally matter whether we do right or wrong, make this stand or basely surrender; faith that death is not a full-stop, but just a comma; faith that there shall be not one lost good, but that all our efforts for righteousness are gathered up into the vast purposes of God.[1]

A Shropshire miner in England went home one night to find that his daughter, very dear to his heart, was dead. In the small Methodist chapel that night his class would meet and wait for him to lead it. And so, eating a hasty meal, he took his little boy by the hand and started for the meeting place. But a storm was brewing in his soul, and for a moment it seemed that his faith would falter. Suddenly he stopped, and, baring his head to the sky while the tears ran down his cheeks, he said:

> Though waves and storms go o'er my head,
> Though strength and health and friends be gone,
> Though joys be withered all and dead,
> Though every comfort be withdrawn,
> On this my steadfast soul relies,
> Father, Thy mercy never dies. [2]

The boy never forgot that, and when he became one of America's greatest preachers, Dr. Parkes Cadman, he told the story and strengthened the faith and thrilled the souls of thousands.

When death comes to a loved one, or when we ourselves knowingly come to that moment, we can cling to the promise of Jesus, the only one who can give us this assurance: "Let not your hearts be troubled; believe in God, believe also in me" (John 14:1, RSV). You and I can know what Paul meant when he wrote of death losing its sting; to the Christian death is only a change, not an end! Eternal life is not limited to some future date or state; it begins here, now. The real life of the Christian is already in heaven. In all of the wonderful truth and beauty of this grand world—in nature, in great music, in friendship, in courage, in the sacrificial love of countless persons all around—I see intimations and glimpses of the other world already here.

God is love. We may now see eternity only as through a glass darkly. But I know that the souls of the righteous are in the hands of God. All we need to know about our loved ones is that they are in God's keeping. The great communion of saints—both in this life and in the life beyond—is held together in the unending love of God. If we live in that communion, we can never be far from each other!

Notes

1. Not Afraid!

1. Hesketh Pearson, *Sir Walter Scott* (New York: Harper & Row, 1954), 244.
2. Hughes Mearns, "The Little Man Who Wasn't There" in *Favorite Poems Old and New,* comp. Helen Ferris (Garden City, N.Y.: Doubleday, 1957), 362.
3. Ralph Waldo Emerson, "Anxiety" in *Masterpieces of Religious Verse,* ed. James Dalton Morrison (New York: Harper & Brothers, 1948), 304.
4. Grace Noll Crowell, *Light of the Years* (New York: Harper & Brothers, 1936), 15.

2. To Be Who I Am

1. G. A. Studdert-Kennedy ["Woodbine Willie," pseud.], *Rough Rhymes of a Padre* (New York: George H. Doran Co., 1918), 27.
2. Talk of the Town, *New Yorker,* Nov. 1, 1982, 33.
3. Lillian Hellman, *The Collected Plays* (Boston: Little, 1972), 583.

5. To Be an Innovator

1. Halford Luccock, *The Acts of the Apostles in Present-Day Preaching* (Chicago: Willett, Clark, 1938), 1:89-90.
2. Margaret B. Kreig, *Green Medicine: The Search for Plants that Heal* (New York: Rand, 1964), 160.
3. *Expository Times* 87 (August 1976):339.

7. To Face the Cross
1. Talk of the Town, *New Yorker*, April 18, 1983, 39.
2. Howard Williams, *Noughts and Crosses* (London: Carey Kingsgate, 1965), 54.
3. Leslie Davison, *Preacher's Gold* (London; Epworth, 1962), 82.
4. James William McClendon, *Biography as Theology* (Nashville: Abingdon, 1974), 127.

8. To Be Alone
1. Albert Edward Day, *An Autobiography of Prayer* (New York: Harper & Brothers, 1952), 171.
2. Wilson O. Weldon, *Mark the Road: Signposts for the Christian Pilgrim* (Nashville: Upper Room, 1973), 76.
3. A. E. Whitham, *The Pastures of His Presence* (London: Hodder and Stoughton, 1939), 294-95.

10. To Face Tomorrow
1. Harry Wilkinson, *The Road of Adventure* (London: Epworth, 1946), 55.

11. To Be a Dreamer
1. G. Ray Jordan, *We Face Calvary—and Life!* (Nashville: Cokesbury, 1936), 113-14.
2. William Barclay, *Daily Celebration* (Waco, Tex.: Word Bks., 1971), 313.
3. Henri J. M. Nouwen, *Gracias!* (San Francisco: Harper & Row, 1983), 59.

12. To Be Afraid
1. J. Wallace Hamilton, *Serendipity* (Westwood, N.J.: Revell, 1965), 65-66.

Epilogue
1. G. T. Bellhouse, *Bread from Heaven* (London: Epworth, 1963), 76.
2. Johann Andrea Rothe, "Now I Found the Ground" in *The Methodist Hymn-Book with Tunes* (London: Methodist Conference Office, 1933),   333.

About the Author

Wilson O. Weldon holds the Bachelor of Divinity degree from Duke University in Durham, North Carolina, and the Doctorate of Divinity degree from High Point College in High Point, North Carolina. Having served numerous churches throughout North Carolina, Dr. Weldon was called to serve as World Editor of The Upper Room from 1967 through 1975. From 1975 through 1981, he was District Superintendent of the Charlotte District of the United Methodist Church. He currently serves as Assistant to the Dean of Duke Divinity School.

During his long and active career, Dr. Weldon has published several books, including *Beyond the Obvious* and *Christmas, More Than a Season*.